True Life Sonnets

Steve Abhaya Brooks

Contents

Sunlight is a Balm

Sunlight is a balm that falls on everything. Orpheus singing
is another balm, along with sleep and curiosity. Stillness
is a dragon with clear eyes. It will drink your thoughts,
until even fear is gone, the same as your balms.

In stillness, you can forget about time and the
fearful events that pass for reality in your dreams.
All your contradictions, wars, and engagements
get pissed away, like so much beer. All temples
of thought, luxury, and lust, are gone in a flash.
1

Common Sanity Has a Fever

Common sanity has a fever like an engine with gas
in its heart, like a fist flung against a stained-glass window,
like digging up dirt in hopes of finding a fortune, like wagging
your tongue in the mirror. Some of us has lost their bearings,
is bewildered, has plants too big for their pots. They sit in
agitated peace, in self-betrayal, in full bloom.

There's always time for second thoughts, but this life
becomes an errand of necessity. Motives die in the night,
born again at dawn. However, when true madness dawns,
it shines, and we wake up from time's deep sleep.

One Good Image

When one's image is dropped from the mirror,
the soul is seen separate from one's gaze.
Seven sins are washed in the reflection,

A sun bird flies into the heat of itself. Trapped
among the feathers, freedom is never lost
in flapping or the heavenly furnace, until
one wanders off from following,
and creation occurs.

This is not juggling or dabbling in talk. It's
not walking on the moon, or driving too fast.
This is muscular song, lying against a
mountain range, one arm along the crest
ridge, the other pulling the wind within.

Here's Our Little One

Here's our little one,
bursting up and out of the atoms,
and here's a thought to chew on;
the last ones out gets to keep their tail,
the rest get pimples and complexes
and a host of delusions.

Here's the low one, the high one,
the middle one, diving in the waterfall,
where the distinctions are lost. Otherwise,
we see the puffed up, the washed away,
the forgotten. Even a small mirror can't
fail to reflect how sad it all seems.

Here's our little one, a swimmer in mirrors,
never forgetting to notice he's also the ocean.
The atoms keep bursting in him, like openings
to the sky, like bubbles, up and out, little pieces
of nothing, that pass into a much bigger nothing,
known or unknown in knowledge and knowing.

Song Transforms the Singer

The bloom is off the rose and wandering all over town.
Fast cars eat up the pavement like blurs of silver and green.
The song transforms the singer. Swollen from nothing into
big things, we get a name, and then someone demands a
story, a rigamarole. Pull back the veil, see small things
swell into big things, in the vast arena of the world.

At the seaside, a great wave of nostalgia washes one's body
back and forth from tub to washboard and onto the clothesline.
Is there a shorter story than this one? Glitzy lights, amusement
parks, the internet, it's all another version of the future of
memory, and then, dissolution.

The Wise One Says

The wise one says there are no wise ones, from
Kathmandu to Mississippi, from the law makers
to the totem carvers, but their music flashes like
fire, even when the fire's gone out, so get here,
before the wash of time swamps us all.

Bright nights and milky days carry death
on their backs. The wise one walks with his
eyes open, behind darkened lids. One way
to cross a bridge is to fly over it.

If you find a golden ring of sand in the desert,
it's a cause for celebration, or another temptation
to ignore celebration for thoughts of enterprise.

No Naked Rumors

Rumor is all there is, until one rumor becomes a bestseller.
Another rumor becomes the source of a thousand rumors.
One rumor gets in hot water, when it begins to tell the truth.
In the desire to organize wonder and necessity into a plan
with a congenial façade, the structure of an airplane
becomes more valued than the embrace of flight.

If you wonder about the paths to enlightenment, are you trying
to get somewhere in yourself, or are you trying to leave yourself
behind, or is it about achieving some perfect and lasting ease
and comfort? Concerned people think they're in charge, or
someone else is. If you're truly naked, all rumors become
rumors of rumors, until they're rumored to be extinct.

Nearer My Life To Thee

Singing Nearer My Life to Thee, with klieg lights
and the sword of Zorro, with women who look like
waves, and sperm whales dashing back and forth
to the supermall.

It's a tragedy when people die, or get married, or have a baby.
It's also an occasion for rejoicing, like harvest time for the heart.
There's no reason to stay in school, when wild music is playing
in the jungles, full of amazing animals, where bloodlust and
jubilation rule the heart, and sensation is outstanding.

You can let the police take care of your problems, your politics,
poverty, storms, sudden wealth, accidents, treachery. Anything
can become either comic, tragic, or both. If you can imagine
peace occurring in your center only when you're dead, you
may as well let the priests take care of your problems,
and your joy, and your love.

The Life of Death

Don't die sooner or later, death is constant.
Death is a ball bouncing from moment to moment.
The underlying moment is what counts, unless
you're bent on counting moments.

It is the nature of death to interrupt living and dying,
to call attention to itself, but death's big vision is without
images. The life of death is a big sky, with new clouds
and more birds than you've ever seen in your life.
The big picture is full of birds flying and dying
among the sudden, evanescent clouds.

A Criminal Mind

I have a criminal mind. Look where I am now.
I'm in a graveyard, and I refuse to be dead in a
world of dread, disturbed by my lack of fear.

I'm a condemned sorcerer, drenched in amazement,
wandering in fire. The old ones are in a bunch, the
young ones are bunched up, their closeness eases
them into wars and disputes, or else it opens
their compassion.

Forgiveness forgets the crimes that are done to it.
I open my mouth, and out comes my own birth
and the birth of the universe. Nothing could
more simply done or more impossible to name.

Climb Any Mountain

Climb any mountain. You might come across a sign that says,
This mountain was built by the mountain builder. Take heed!
But you took heed, you took steps, you bought a jacket, you
took pictures, you took time to write in your journal.

You see the stars floating in a purple sky, like bright lights
cast against an ebony night, like millions of tiny flames in
a vast motionless lake, but there's a shadow on the water
that claims credit for your comparisons, even as you
wonder where comparison and credit came from.

If everything you ever thought was real, was made real
within the eye of your mind, how could you not feel
grateful, whether or not you ever thought there was a
builder of anything?

Here's a Toast

Here's to a well-constructed Podcast,
with love and war and fashion, and pretty faces,
among the pics of struggle, triumph, and defeat.

Forgive me, but we must have been lovers in a previous life,
said one wave to another, as they were pulled back from the shore,
as their dramatic features become indistinguishable from the sea,
before and after their birth astounds the shore, once more.

Rain is everywhere, like music and parts of the night,
that merge and withdraw from even darker parts of the night,
until the morning's light makes night a musical memory.

Here's a handful of something. China produces them,
so does Nebraska. These handfuls appear everywhere.
Holding them is common, letting go is less so.

A Rolling Apple

A rolling apple, a peach on a branch, a peeled banana, a pear,
appear like rain falling from a human structure, like images
put together from a lovely or an unlovely afternoon.

Let's be kind, it's a gift. A pool of water may not stay
a pool for very long. Even a tree will fly away, if you
wait long enough.

Miracles are common, but the one who sees a miracle and calls it
common is the true miracle. Look at the marble in our mountains
of marble. Look at the marvels in our marvellousness. They are
diaphanous, transparent and thick, like a giant brick Trojan horse,
empty of war. Build your house into a home free from the Trojans
and their rolling war machines shaped like toy animals.

Toss Me a Flower

Toss me a flower, a wine bottle, some fruit, sprinkle my night
with lights, toss a hat on my head, throw a pair of pants on my legs,
glare at me in reproach, the world is sickly sore. Eden is a graveyard.
You can only stack so many bodies in one place, and pretty soon,
it's not the same old paradise.

The language of the heart calls for fewer and fewer syllables.
No one broke his leg today, no one spilled anything hot, not
one homemaker had a problem, every skier made it down
the mountain. Who's to blame when nothing is wrong?

Standing atop the Himalayas lends one no particular
advantage in love, so the next time you reach the top,
plant a kiss on the sky.

Music in the Summertime

I'm shown what I imagine, or is it the other way around?
Or might it be both, with no difference between them?
Does music rise in the summer, or does summer rise
in the music, or do we rise, like music in the summertime?

If I'm wearing an ugly color the day I die, will I then be free
of such petty concerns? And what about now, in my choice
of colors? The most serene landscape appears on the same
screen as Death's Dormitory. If I wear bright colors the day
before my funeral, maybe I'll forget to remember death.

Flying Up the Down Ramp

As a diligent self-examiner, use your fingers. Pull the flesh apart,
looking for worms. Among some, it's a social bonding ritual.

With the skill of a physician with bedroom eyes, the intensity
transfers from internal to external, from gangrene to the Ganges
to Gangnam. There's an endless parade of glamorous strangers,
cars, trucks, livestock, angels, and swimsuit models.

Breathe it all in, as deep as you can, and then breathe it all out.
The cattle, cars and trucks, the strangers, angels and models,
will keep coming, as long as there are paths from there to here
and here to there.

Everyone is a Fountain

Everyone is a fountain of glory, worms, and regeneration, clever names
for the kids, genocide, inspiration, helmet laws, ways to drink beer, words
that sing, table manners, bad jokes, international conferences, and folk art.
Yet one's interest in these things seems worn down in time.

First, someone invented the piano, and by now, you'd think every song
would sound the same, yet we keep hearing original music. Perhaps the ear
chooses to remember what it wants, or the mind is easily fooled, or delight
stays fresh in the mind, as wonder transforms the mundane.

The temperature of the sun cools as it reaches the edge
and then inexplicably heats up, just like you and me.

Heroes Are Not New

If you want to know the truth, dance. Put on the shirt of your truth,
and then rip it off, before you can remember your name, and dance.

The way the ear works is no concern to the ear, though it may assist
in the ear's discovery. Don't give your machinery a pet name. Heroes
are not new. Drowning doesn't surprise the ocean. Birds fly up and
dig a hole in the sky. Simple joy is revolutionary. Arrest yourself
in joy, even as you commit all the other petty crimes of the heart.

The Biggest Ranch

Even the biggest ranch has a fence around it, with cars on
blocks, and religious volunteers knocking on the door. Its
estate is surrounded by flying bugs and so-called wild horses.

We are Macadam, married to asphalt. Our children mate
with creatures rom outer space, in this dust-mote-memory,
forest-primeval among the stars. Despite sand dunes in the
mind, wind storms in the heart, spirit is never deranged.

Master of the Dream

Forget everything I say, my love. Better yet, forget what
I say, before I say it. I guarantee you'll fall in love with me
and my words. This trick works just as well on all the other
poet/lovers.

Forget everything, right before it occurs, forget everyone,
just before you meet them. Forget love itself, and love
will be your legacy, and you will be its originator.

Every other animal is blessed with this forgetting, except
you, Master of the Horses, Master of the Fields, Master
of the Dream, except you, Master of the Mystery.
Now is your chance to outdo them all.

Secret Rumbling

Secret rumbling is my nature, along with a rumbling generosity.
I rumble in the most generous way, nearly always in secret. It's
natural for me to vulcanize, without fanfare, often in private
and still willing to give generously of the innate self
I was born to form islands from.

I am a singer, quietly, au natural, with a song in my heart,
open to the wind, the sun, the sky, the stars. Hidden mostly,
I teach my untaught, unteachable being to all those I meet.
I erupt, I flow, I scald, I burn. Let me burn until I have
become an oasis in the sea.

I Hear Three Songs

I hear three songs, from three birds, singing three times.
One bird keeps time for the others. Their harmony
delights them all.

Here comes a hunter. Bang, the birds are dead. This is a sad
homage to beauty and a paltry version of myth. The old time
poets never really cared about urns or birds or even words.

Talk is a row of candles. Poetry is a row of light.
Love itself is a row of no rows.

Once Upon a Time

My ambition has always been to fly over the lands
and the waters of the earth and weave them into a sea
and landscape, just as they are.

I saw the face of Jesus among lichen, not a lichen Jesus,
but Jesus rising like any one might from a pond or a pool,
with his hair slicked back and his eyes closed, then open.
He smiled and then he winked, and then he sank again.

I have dreamt of flying above the earth and folding
the four directions into every moment and every place
as they are now, at any imagined crossroads. I fly above
and see myself below, looking up. I see myself, above,
without ever leaving my eyes.

This Muddle of Muds

You could say that nothing is real. You could invent things
to fill the void. You could call this life a crazy box. We know
we live in a fascinating, distracting reality. There are swells
in the river and uncertain royalty. There are friendship rings
and groping animals. There are gods who revere and reveal
themselves. There are flights of fancy gone into a hard stall.
There are stronger drugs and all night kennels. There are ala
carte tales and overlapping stories in this life, on this earth,
in this muddle of muds.

This mud abhors a vacuum and loads it up with swellings,
caterwauling, overturned refrigerators, a fortress mentality.
In this surfeit of disorders, this leaning tower of babble, this
messenger service, this overweening language, this tick school,
wonder is never far away, in this inevitable slide from nothing
to something and back again.

One of the Mysteries

One mystery of poetry is to sing the empty air,
until one is free to the ocean, wide beneath the words.
In the beginning, we don't like poetry, until it starts
to sound like something, and then we take relief in its
verisimilitude. Then we despise routine and begin
to die, until death and birth are green again.

In the life and death song everything rhymes with
everything else. Each breath is ripped asunder by
wonder. To disguise while revealing, these bundles
of old words are born anew, wordless in their beauty.

Swift Kiss of Night

Swift kiss of night, you win the reach of life,
you concede to conquer. Eternity sings the heart
of stillness. I sit in an empty chair outside
the door that opens itself.

True Life
Sonnets
Steve Abhaya
Brooks

ISBN: 9798883789334
copyright 2024
Abhaya Books & Art
1 Battle Sq. Apt. 602
Asheville, NC 28801
steve@steveabhaya.com

Made in the USA
Columbia, SC
13 March 2024